WELCOME

to the

REAL WORLD!!

All materials in this book are Copyright and Trademark protected.

Preface

My goal for writing this book is to help reduce the number of hair salon failures.

Since the early 1990's I have been building successful businesses. First in the securities industry in the form of broker dealer, trading and high technology companies. In the early 2000's, I began building successful businesses within the salon and spa industry. Owning a successful business can be rewarding on two primary levels: financial and emotional. These two "rewards" can be hugely fulfilling. The financial reward helps you pay the bills, keep the business going and allows you to do things such as vacation, pay for school or simply to "live". Emotional rewards give you interpersonal security. It gives you confidence in life. Isn't this what we are seeking when we decide to open our own business? Our own hair salon?

Yet, salons fail. Just drive around your neighborhood and beyond; you will realize this is true. Some salons open quietly and close just as quietly. Failure is unfortunately entirely too prevalent in this industry and that is the purpose of this book: *Reduce hair salon failures!* There can be nothing more devastating than seeing the hope drain from a salon owner's face and it happens all the time. Venturing into owning a salon didn't start that way.

Failure is painful; physically, psychologically and financially. It causes you to freeze up and forget who, what and why you are. I have met with many salon owners who have either failed or are/were on the brink of failure. It's no fun; in fact, it's very, very sad. I am grateful for my successes as a business owner. None of them came easy and all required a great amount of time, hard work, passion and dedication. With every business I've started, I never forgot the fact that businesses fail and kept it my mantra that failure was never going to be an option. Through these successes and by keeping failure in my rear view mirror, I have learned a great deal about what does and does not work within the hair salon industry. I have learned, like almost everything you do in life, there are processes that will lead you to your ultimate destination. Starting a new business is just one of those ventures. Simply building your dream into a viable venture requires numerous steps, processes and systems, if you dare to succeed.

I'm constantly aghast at the number of failures that all small businesses experience. I'm appalled at the number of hair salons that fail. Building a business and hoping (or praying) it will succeed is not a good system to rely upon if you wish to succeed. You can pray; you can hope, you can even go visit the local fortune teller, but none of these means will cause you to become successful in your new business venture. It's just not that simple. And it clearly has not worked for me anytime I play the lottery. I pray, I hope, I even pop open fortune cookies looking for the exact one that is going to guarantee me a grand, lotto win; but it never happens.

Building a successful business cannot be equated to playing the lotto. There is entirely too much at stake. The ticket to "open a business" costs a lot more than $1 and the risks can be high. I will never dismiss "luck" but it's impossible to quantify and predict when or if you will ever experience the luck phenomenon. The only certain way to succeed in business is to implement systems that have a proven track record and to be fully cognizant of every aspect of your business. If you are unable to be cognizant, then be sure to have a trusted soul at the helm of your salon. The shore is rocky and running into shallow water can only lead to one thing: grounding the ship and failing at your business.

In the case of the hair stylist who decides to open their own hair salon, it takes much more than knowing how to cut and color hair to own and operate your own hair salon. Cutting hair simply does not qualify you to be an owner; yet over 90% of hair salons are owned by hair stylists. There is a vast gap between being an industry technician and being a small business owner. The hair stylist who decides to own, knows little to nothing about how to run a business and with 90% of these styling geniuses eventually owning, failure is more the norm than the rarity.

It's time to change that statistic. In the U.S. alone there are over 500,000 hair salon establishments. Over 450,000 are owned by hair stylists. Each year over 10% fail. That's over 45,000 hair salons per year that fail. Let me repeat: 45,000 hair salon business failures every single year. And that doesn't even include the failures from the non-hair stylist owned hair salons and these are conservative numbers. OUCH! Yet every year, new salons are opened and with cosmetology schools graduating stylists in record numbers. It's easy to see that salon openings will continue to propagate and with those openings, a proliferation of hair salon failures.

Imagine if each of these salons employed just three people (most employ significantly more); this means over 150,000 individuals per year will lose their jobs. Truth is, the number is actually higher. It's not my goal to scare anyone one away, however, the point has to be made. Hair salons fail and they fail all the time. The overall affects of failure are far reaching. They go beyond just you. Failure adversely affects everyone: staff, third-party vendors, the guest and your community.

Failure can cause irreparable damage to your health and personal relationships. It's time we take care of our businesses much the same way we take care of ourselves (most of us anyway). Keep the business healthy by paying attention to every aspect of the business. Maintain a sense of urgency with everything that you do. You'll be glad that you did. This sense of urgency will keep you and everyone you have surrounded yourself with sharp and on your toes. Lazy leadership cannot exist if your business is to exist.

This book is about providing anyone interested in owning their own hair salon a road map to their own success. Failure can never be an option, but you must always keep it in your rear view mirror to avoid it. Never assume you cannot fail. Never assume that "if you build it, they will come". Welcome to the real world of small business ownership.

Throughout this book, I will provide you with systems to implement throughout the lifecycle of opening your own hair salon beginning with the dream and ending with the reality. It's my goal and my intentions to either dissuade you completely from heading down the ownership path (at least for now) or to do everything I can to mirror your dream with reality. As you might imagine, this isn't such a simple task based on how many hair salons will fail this year and next and every year following. But it can be done because it HAS been done.

Some of the most successful salons in the world are none-other than the salons whose names we all recognize and all fall under a single category called franchised salons. Franchised businesses in general are significantly more successful than their independently owned counterparts. This is true regardless of industry, but especially in the hair salon industry. 50% of every small business fails in 5 years yet 90% of all franchised businesses remain in business by year 7! Why?

Successful businesses have proven systems in place to assure their success.

Truth is, failure can happen for numerous reasons: lack of capital, knowledge, customers, staff, health or family issues. This list could go on. But in small business, and this will encompass most of the above, failures occur due to a lack of systems that address planning, staffing, customers, education and family issues. Franchise companies are all systems based; at least the successful ones.

What is evidently missing in the hair salon industry are systems that can and should be shared with those 90% of all salon owners and future salon owners. Systems that hair salon franchisors won't share with you and for good reason. Franchisors have paid hundreds of thousands of dollars developing the systems that make their business successful. Further, they have gone down the path of trial and error; live and learn, etc and now want to profit from their knowledge. And that's ok because due to these diligent entrepreneurs, more business owners have become successful, albeit within the franchise system they have purchased; but again, that's ok.

Franchise salons represent less than 6% of all hair salons in the United States. This book is for all the other 94% and even more so, for the future 94%; those who have yet to take that giant leap into small business ownership. Success can never be guaranteed; even in the franchise world. However, by having access to the same or similar systems that franchised salons have in place, your chances of success are increased significantly. And this assumes you adhere to the systems.

Success

=

passion + dedication + hard work + knowledge

This book is dedicated to your success. I sincerely hope that from these pages you will learn more about the steps necessary to be a successful hair salon owner and perhaps a little bit more about yourself in the process.

TO YOUR SUCCESS!!

Acknowledgments

There is no way I could ever put to paper the words contained in this book without the experiences and relationships I have gained in my life. When I graduated from high school, an older gentleman I refer to as my mentor gave me this advice: "Matt" he said, "life's a game; play to win"! Those words have stuck with me all my life but somewhere along the line I mixed in a high level of integrity, accountability and responsibility to those words. People have come and gone in my life. For those who remain, they have done so for a reason. This will be true for all of you. The experiences you glean out of life will shape you into who you are today and who you will become tomorrow. My advice is to never burn a bridge (its a certainty you will regret that sometime in your life) and, if you can take the time to a job twice, do it right the first time. I have harvested many experiences in my life. Many are personal and many had to do with businesses. There are entirely too many people to thank so suffice it to say I won't "name, names" but would simply say thank you to my friends, my family, to a litany of peers and to everyone who took the time to guide me in my life.

Much of the factual information in this book came from my own personal experiences whether it was I who had the experience or through others who were close to me. Facts and numbers came from a variety of sources which include the Professional Beauty Association, U.S.Census Bureau, the U.S. Bureau of Labor Statistics and the Small Business Association. The Internet is a great tool for gleaning all kinds of information but it's important to verify its validity and accuracy and to the very best of my knowledge, I have done so for these pages.

As you go forth towards owning your own hair salon, remember, it's ok to lean on your friends and family for advice and help. You may not always like what you hear, but differing perspectives will help you make the right decisions; both in business and in life. So remember, "life's a game, play to win, but win honestly and with integrity".

Chapter One

Salon Ownership: Are you wearing Rose Colored Glasses?

The 20-million dollar question you need to ask yourself is: "Is owning my own hair salon the right move for me"? There are good reasons to consider owning your own hair salon and there are poor reasons. What are your reasons? Is the timing right to begin thinking about owning? Truth is, there is never a bad or a good time, it really just depends on your level of desire and commitment. And whether you can actually make it happen will depend on being able to fund the project.

As a segue into considering opening your own hair salon, think about "why" you want to open the salon. What drives you to even contemplate this decision? Generally, businesses first think about "what" they do or will do, then "how" they do it and finally, "why" they do it. Traditional thinking takes you down this path. Break from tradition!

Therefore, rather than thinking about what you do and how you do it, you should spend time contemplating "Why"? As the world is acutely aware, there are hair salons all over the place. Sometimes salons are directly adjacent to or across the street from other salons. Does the world need yet another hair salon? We all know "what" a salon does and we generally understand "how" they do the "what". But why do you want to own your own salon? A good exercise is to jot down all the pro's and con's of owning your own business. Think of the reasons you   love   the business; what do you dislike; what will you do differently compared to any other salon? How will your business impact your community, the environment, your staff   and you? Anything and everything that comes to mind, put to paper. Why is the single most important question you will answer about opening your new salon. It reflects the genuine purpose of your business.

Once you have created your list, put it away for a day or two. After a period of "rest", revisit the list. Can you add anything further? Are there notes you might remove? Start to really think about WHY you want to own your own hair salon.

Owning your own business can be a great experience and a liberating experience as well. Being in charge of your own destiny is very powerful and can lead to both financial freedom and eventually more freedom of time. These things can only become a reality if:

1. You have experience running a business,

2. You are able to gain the education to guide you through the processes

3. OR, you choose to own a franchised system where a team of experts will assist you *almost* every step of the way.

The reason I say almost, is that no one will do the work for you. Ultimately, is up to you. However, if you have a great salon concept, are willing to invest the necessary blood, sweat and tears, have a great opportunity and the appropriate dose of passion to go with it, then you will be well on your way to owning and operating your own successful hair salon business. But, don't be fooled and PLEASE, *take the rose colored glasses off* before you begin your journey. Running a successful hair salon is not the same as being a great hair stylist, which we have said before. The requirements to be a licensed cosmetologist, regardless of the state where you reside, hardly qualify or prepare you to own and operate a living and breathing hair salon. In a business, such as the hair salon industry, there are dozens of moving parts that the successful business owner must contend with on a daily basis. Each of these moving parts is an integral part of your business and if you are to succeed it's important to fully understand the amount of attention each of these requires.

These parts include establishing the business in the first place and everything that is involved with that process. Once the business is open, you need to manage a team of stylists and perhaps guest service staff; you need to market your salon, keep track of inventory, payroll, registrations, cleaning, purchasing and the list goes on from here.

A great number of people dream of one day owning their own business. Isn't that the American dream after all? Or is it the American nightmare? Before you venture out and start your own salon, you need to ask yourself some important questions and then put some serious thought into every aspect of your business and why you chose to open it.

Start with: "Will this business make me"? "Or break me"?

So the real question you must ask yourself is: **Why?**
Would your answers be:

-   *To make a lot of money.*

-   *To spend more time with my family.*

-   *Less work to do as the owner.*

-   *no one telling me what to do and how to do it.*

-   *I want to own the business but not be active with the business.*

If any of these are the sole reasons for starting your own business, you may want to think again. Business ownership is clearly, and I do mean clearly, not for you.

Yet, if you start your hair salon for the following reasons, you have a stronger chance of succeeding and a significantly greater chance of loving what you are doing.

-   You are passionate about the industry and the business you intend to start.

-   You strongly believe in the salon you intend to open and know that your services would satisfy a genuine need in your community or the market as a whole.

-   You have the mental stamina to own your own business and understand the concept that there is no such thing as a "straight line"

-   You are determined, you have drive, you have a lot of patience and you can maintain a positive attitude even under adverse conditions.

-   You do not fear failure but maintain the attitude that failure is not an option.

-   You are detail oriented and flourish as an independent. You are a take charge type of person and can apply both intelligent and creative solutions to problems that come your way.

-   You are a people person. You are able to get along with almost anyone. This is, after-all, a people business

- You are honest, healthy, have a high level of integrity and are goal oriented.

- You understand that this is your salon and you must be active in the day-to-day operations of the business.

Although there is never a guarantee of success for any business, if you can satisfy several, if not all of the above, your chances of operating a successful hair salon increase substantially. Remember, this is your business not your staff's, but yours, so do unto it as you want your business to do unto you. Treat it with respect and a high level of awareness. Be flexible and able to change or make changes when market conditions require it. And always maintain an open mind. This doesn't mean you flow with every new idea that comes your way, but if the business isn't working, be willing to figure out why and make any necessary adjustments.

There are many reasons for a business to fail and the top reasons are poor management, under-capitalization and lack of systems implementation. Most new business owners lack the business and management knowledge that is germane to operating a business in general. This knowledge includes but is certainly not limited to the following:

- Finance and accounting: knowing your numbers.

- Location-location; don't ignore its importance

- People management-guests, staff and family

- Human resources-interviewing, hiring, employee manuals

- Marketing-You've built it, now you need to assure "they will come"

- Inventory for retail and professional use

- Time management-balance in life and in business

It's important to fully understand not just your strengths, but your weaknesses as well. If you fail to recognize this from the start, failure may become imminent. It's ok to not be an expert regarding every aspect of your business at first. You are not alone. This is the way it is with almost every business large and small. It doesn't excuse you from creating the right team to help you manage all the moving parts of your salon or taking the time to truly become intimate with not just your business, but your industry as well. Again, this is YOUR business so be in it. Be an active part of the day-to-day operations. Even if you're not keeping the books, it's up to you to understand them completely. Even though you may not have graphic art skills, you need to review and approve every ad that has been created for your business. Again, this is your business.

Never let fear deter you from venturing forward. Fear can be a real show stopper and most of the time for illogical reasons. We are all a little scared   when we venture into something we are not 100% familiar with. You are not alone. If you are a hair stylist, do you remember that very first hair cut on a very real client? I'm sure a certain level of fear gripped you when you made that first cut. It's ok to be scared but it's not ok to let fear get in the way of making the right decisions. Fear can never be an excuse for not addressing a problem or decisions you will need to make. But know that it's ok to have certain levels of trepidation.

Chapter Two

Dream to Reality

It's easy to dream. We all do it. By virtue of the fact that you are reading this book, your dream is to own your own hair salon. Let's take that back. Your dream is to own your own "successful" hair salon. Taking your dream and making it a reality is a myriad of steps. As a salon owner, this responsibility will be a full time job which means, if you are a hair stylist, that "stylist" hat must come off and the new "owner" hat must now be worn. To be very blunt: Hair stylists who work behind the chair in their own salon have already set themselves up for failure. The only exception to this is if the stylist owner hires a qualified manager to "manage" the day to day operations; but this adds a new expense to your bottom line. Or, if you own a one person shop.

How an owner thinks relative to how a hair stylist thinks is like comparing night to day. For example, hair stylist knows how they get paid. And how they get paid is vastly different from how an owner gets paid. Therefore, to be paid as an owner, you must think like an owner; you must behave like an owner; you must manage like an owner. This is the **RULE! OBEY IT!** Or accept the fact that the likelihood of your salon succeeding is now vastly diminished. The responsibilities of an owner are also vastly different than those of a hair stylist. As a stylist you may have superficial responsibilities when it come to salon operations such as back bar inventory or supplies, but as the owner, this is ultimately your responsibility, along with every other aspect of the salon.

If you still want to work behind the chair, then you must think long and hard about WHY you want to own your own salon. You could just as easily rent space, work for yourself and not take on the responsibility of not just your life, but the lives you will bring into your business including staff and guests. It's literally impossible to run a busy hair salon if the majority of your time is spent behind the chair. There is no sense owning a hair salon if the money you earn for yourself is generated from the services you provide by being behind the chair. Businesses require constant and ongoing attention. If most of your time is spent behind the chair then who is really behind the business?

If your dream is to own your own salon and create opportunities for others, AND you are ready to step away from behind the chair, then this book and program is for you. The systems included here will be a guide towards owning your own hair salon. Salon success will be your responsibility, so as an owner, let's get started.

Owning your own salon can be an incredibly rewarding and inspiring venture. You are now the leader of your own destiny and the destiny of many others who will one day come through your business, either as a member of your accomplished and professional staff or as a guest who wouldn't dream of taking their business anywhere else. Think about that. ANYWHERE ELSE! Let your passion breath life into this new business and lead that passion with a good dose of love but always maintain a sense of responsibility and accountability to the financial health of your business.

This is your business. Always remember that. As a new business owner you will learn to wear a great number of hats. You will wear the sweep hair hat, empty trash hat, count cash hat, wash windows and mirrors hat, be empathetic and sometimes sympathetic; you will be a leader and take that role seriously, but with a healthy sense of compassion. Yet as the owner of this business you will pay close attention to your revenues and the bills you pay. You will pay close attention to staffing and the attitudes the team brings into your salon. You will be confident yet humble. Your integrity will guide you and you will always be accountable for your actions and the actions of everyone within your salon.

You will pay attention to today, but always be looking towards the future. As you begin to settle into wearing the owner hat versus the hair stylist hat, the differences will unfold and become extremely evident why stylists rarely become successful salon owners. The dream is much different than the reality or at least the pathway to living that dream successfully is quite different.

So how do you get from the dream of owning a hair salon to the reality of owning a hair salon? Just like Dorothy in the Wizard of Oz when she followed the Yellow Brick Road, you need to follow the road toward successful salon ownership. It might seem scary at times and overwhelming at others. But the path is there, right in front of you. You just have to follow it. So let's start taking some steps.

To start, you will need to draft a business plan. The business plan is your road map. As a part of this plan, you will need to develop certain financial spreadsheets to determine if your salon can make money. You will hire an accountant to look after you, financially. After that you will determine a location, hire an architect and a builder. You will form the legal entity for your salon and obtain all legal registrations. Yes, there is much to do between your dreaming of owning and actually opening your new salon.

As you begin this process of determining if owning a salon is right for you, you will begin to realize how much time goes into the daily operations of the salon. You will begin to understand that operating your salon leaves you very little time to spend time behind the chair. It will become clearly evident that for your salon to succeed, owning and operating is a full time job and not something you can just "wing" from behind the chair. Success is tantamount and therefore every effort needs to be provided towards succeeding. As we have stated, failures are very prevalent in the hair salon industry and the majority of those failures are due to owners remaining behind the chair rather than there business. The sooner hair stylists come to this conclusion, the sooner there will be a reduction in salon failures.

Keep in mind, however, that just because you change your hat from stylist to owner doesn't guarantee success. There are many steps, as we also mentioned earlier, that you must follow and pay close attention to for you to have a bona fide chance of succeeding. Remember, you can succeed. Despite the plethora of salon failures, there are a great many that succeed but it takes more than desire and luck. It takes many hours a week of dedicated loyalty to your business. It take always keeping your eye on the salons financial health. It takes having a plan and sticking to that plan. It takes making tough decisions and it also means accepting the fact that not every decision you make is going to be accepted favorably by your staff. But these decisions must and will be made for the overall benefit of the business which in turn will benefit your staff. Being a good owner, driven towards success is never about winning a popularity contest. However, when the decisions you have made prove themselves out in the form of operating a successful hair salon, staff will become dedicated disciples of your business. There is, after all, something to be said about working for and with a winning team.

Chapter Three

Step One: The Business Plan

No business will ever get far without a Business Plan or "BP". This is the bible for every successful business regardless of industry. Unfortunately, all too many hair salon owners neglect the importance of this document. You will NOT make that mistake. Before you invest any dollars, you must draft a business plan.

The business plan is the best *first* step you will take towards determining if owning a hair salon is the *right* step for you. The process of taking all the thoughts you have about owning and putting them to paper can be a very defining moment. This process will be the first and best way for you to become intimate with the proposed business you desire to own. Developing your business plan is a very exciting time. As an artist, this is the document you will begin to meld your own creativity with the business aspects of owning and operating a successful hair salon.

The business plan defines your intentions for your new hair salon. It's the road map for your business. The business plan is also necessary for many reasons. It's necessary to raise capital for your new endeavor. Whether you need to take a bank loan or raise capital through private investors (which includes friends and family members).

Imagine you are in Miami and given the task to find the address: 23467 53rd Avenue N.E. in Seattle. However, you are not allowed to use a map, a GPS or any other means of navigation (except for the stars at night). Will you ever reach your destination? If so, how long will it take? How efficient will you be in arriving at the final address? The answer is; not very efficient, assuming you arrive at the address at all. The business plan is this road map so be as detailed as possible when drafting it.

No one will lend you a dime or invest into your company if you do not have a business plan. You will not be able to open a bank account without a business plan. As stated in the above example, you won't know how to get from point "A" to point "B" without a business plan. This will be the single most important document for your business, so plan on spending quality time drafting it in intimate detail.

The business plan consists of several critical components which are described in the following pages.

Executive Summary
The Executive Summary is the first section of your business plan but will be the last part that you draft. Generally, the Executive Summary should not exceed two pages. The Executive Summary needs to be to the point and describe a summary of the plan that follows. One page is preferred by most investors and banks.

Include everything that you would cover in a five-minute interview or as the expression goes in your "elevator" pitch. Explain the fundamentals of the proposed business: What will your services be? Hair cutting, coloring; every service that will be provided in the salon. What product lines will you carry and why? Who will your customers be? Where will they come from? List all of the owners. What do you think the future holds for your salon and the hair industry? Make it enthusiastic, professional, complete, and concise. The Executive Summary will be the single most important part of the business plan you will write and the reason is that from the Executive Summary, interest in your project will be derived. Make it POP! If applying for a loan, state learly how much you want, precisely how you are going to use the funds and how the money will make your business more profitable, thereby ensuring repayment. This is important because whoever lends you the money will want to be repaid and anyone who invests into your salon will want to know it's a good investment.

General Salon Description
Who are you, what do you do and why? This is where you really get to introduce your salon concept. Dial in on you, your experience, what's going to separate you and your salon from everyone else. Talk about your location and your culture. You can also talk about what products you plan to use and retail and why.

Products and Services
Write about the products you will use professionally and retail within the salon. What sets theses products apart from the rest of the competition? List the services your salon will provide here as well. Is there anything that is truly unique about the product lines you will use

and sell that will be advantageous to your business? Or the services you will offer?

Competitive Analysis

Know your competition. Remember, guests will travel almost any distance for quality hair care services but only if you have set yourself above and beyond your competition. So, when doing this analysis, create demographic rings of 1 mile, 3 miles and 5 miles. What salons or spas will you compete against with your salon? What will set you apart from these other salons or spas? Your competitors will include other salons, spas and retail outlets that will retail the same products that you will be retailing.

This competitive analysis will also help you dial in on your service pricing and might even dictate what products you will ultimately retail and use within your salon.

Revenue Sources

Some say this is where the rubber hits the road. How will you make money? List every possible means by which your salon will generate revenues. These should include all service related revenues, retail, other products such as clothing, jewelry, art, etc. List all your services from cutting to coloring to waxing to skin care if your salon provides that service. Leave nothing out! You may have a passion for the industry but never forget that you are also in the business to make money.

Marketing Plan

Before you even sign a lease for your new salon, how do you plan to market it? Remember, "if you build it they will come" only works in Hollywood, not in the real world of hair salon ownership. All potential guests need to know where you are located and should understand why you, versus any of your competitors should be their salon. Think about your budget, where can you advertise the most effectively. Where can you advertise for the least cost yet with the greatest, positive impact on your business? Full page ads in beautiful glossy magazines look great, but might cost more for a single ad than you might spend for 12 months worth of advertising elsewhere. Be smart about how and where you spend your money. And don't forget about the Internet and all its power!

This sounds simple, but be intelligent on how you plan to market your salon. Before putting this section together, do some research. What media types are available and what are the costs associated with using these differing medias. These might include newspapers, magazines, radio, TV, local churches, chambers of commerce or the Internet. Don't simply list marketing ideas without learning about each. You need to speak competently about where and why you will market your new salon through different media types. Remember also, think about a budget here.

Market research - Why?

No matter how great your salon may be, the business cannot succeed without effective marketing. And this begins with careful, systematic research. It is very dangerous to assume that you already know about your intended market and its surrounding demographics. You need to do market research to make sure you're on track. Use the business planning process as your opportunity to uncover data and to question your marketing efforts. Your time will be well spent.

Market research - How?

There are two kinds of market research: primary and secondary. Secondary research means using published information such as industry profiles, trade journals, newspapers, magazines, census data, and demographic profiles. This type of information is available in public libraries, industry associations, chambers of commerce, from vendors who sell in the salon industry and from government agencies such as the U.S. Departments of Labor and the U.S. Census Bureau. But the best place to find data you seek will be found on the Internet. The caveat is being able to verify the information you find. There are more online sources than you could possibly use. Your chamber of commerce has good information on the local area. Trade associations and trade publications, such as the Professional Beauty Association and the Green Book will have excellent salon industry-specific data. Speak with local distributors as well. They have, after all, seen it all.

Primary research means gathering your own data. For example, you could do your own vehicular or pedestrian traffic count at a proposed salon location, use the yellow pages to identify competitors and conduct surveys or focus-group interviews to learn about consumer preferences. Professional market research can be very costly, but through the Internet, there are many web sites that show small business owners how to do effective research or will provide the data you seek.

In your marketing plan, be as specific as possible; give statistics, numbers, and sources for your information. The marketing plan will be the basis, later on, of the all-important sales projections when developing your initial cash flow spreadsheets.

Talk about what you will do to give back to your community. Community giving will be one of the best means to market your hair salon. Always remember to give generously and shout it out loud. Don't be shy; let the world know what you are doing and why!

Remember, if you can't talk about your new salon, then who can?
BE VOCAL!

Operational Plan
Outline staffing, hours of operation, days open or closed, etc. Will you be the manager or will you need to hire a manager? Will you hire guest service staff to answer phones, book appointments, check guests in and out, etc or will those responsibilities belong to you or your professional (styling) staff? The bottom line here is, how will your business operate? Will it be different than other similar salons? Be detail oriented here. Outline here as well how you will pay your staff. This will have a big impact on not just your projected financials but on hiring staff as well.

Management and Organization
Who will manage the business on a day-to-day basis? What experience do you or a prospective manager bring to the business? What special or distinctive competencies does the manager of your salon have if that person is not you? What plans will you have in place if this person is lost or incapacitated? What if this person is you? As an owner, these are important items to think through.

Outline each position you will be staffing within the salon. These positions might include the differing levels of hair stylists, guest services, management or owner. Who is responsible for overseeing these positions? Will it be you? A manager or a peer? Assign responsibilities within your salon. Include position descriptions for key employees. If you are seeking loans or investors, include resumes of yourself and key employees.

List all professional and advisory support individuals such as your accountant, attorney, insurance agent and banker.

Personal Financial Statement
No bank or credible lending or leasing company will consider lending you the funds necessary to build your salon without a personal financial statement. This will provide insight to these institutions as to the financial health and responsibility of you personally. 99.% of every loan or lease made to you for your business will be personally guaranteed by you. If you are not credit worthy, then it will become highly unlikely that you will ever obtain the funds necessary to open your new hair salon.
A personal financial statement will provide two pieces of information: How much money you make from all sources and how many bills you pay monthly. Include everything. Lenders will find out anyway when they run a credit check on you.

Sales Projections and Cash Flows
Based on your products and services and your operational plan, we know where you will generate revenues, but how much? Sales projections and cash flow statements will determine if your salon will be a financially viable business. Many factors will determine these projections such as location, staffing, number of chairs, hours of operation and cost of services provided.

Cash flows will include all cash on hand, all projected revenues and then deduct all operating expenses. The big question will be: "Is there any cash left over"? Businesses rarely ever turn a profit or are cash flow positive from the beginning. This generally takes time as you begin to "ramp-up" your new business. Because of this, it's very important to have a reasonable amount of cash on hand to give you the necessary cushion while you establish your new salon.

As a rule of thumb, after all costs associated with opening your salon have been paid and you have dialed in on reasonable sales projections; you should have anywhere between 10-15% of your 12 month sales revenue projections in cash to start your business. For example: If you project gross revenues of $300,000, plan to have in cash when you start, $30-$45K in extra operating capital. Most businesses fail because they are under capitalized right from the start. Make sure this does NOT happen to you!

Startup Expenses and Capitalization

You will have many expenses before you even begin operating your new hair salon. It's important to estimate these expenses accurately and then to plan where you will get sufficient capital. This is a research project, and the more thorough your research efforts, the less chance that you will leave out important expenses or underestimate them.

Even with the best of research, however, opening a new hair salon has a way of costing more than you anticipate. There are two ways to make allowances for surprise expenses. The first is to add a little "padding" to each item in the budget. The problem with that approach, however, is that it destroys the accuracy of your carefully written plan. The second approach is to add a separate line item, called contingencies, to account for the unforeseeable. After you determine your total expenses, you might add an extra 15-20% for contingencies. This is the approach we recommend.

In a later chapter, I provide a table with a list of expense items you will have for your new salon. It will be a guide as you research the furniture and fixtures you will need to open your new hair salon.

Explain your research and how you arrived at your forecasts of expenses. Give sources, amounts, and terms of proposed loans. In the event you bring on investors, explain in detail how much will be contributed by each investor and what percent ownership each will have.

Financials

The financial plan consists of a 36 month sales projection, a cash-flow projection, a projected balance sheet and a break-even calculation. Together they constitute a reasonable estimate of your company's financial future. More important, the process of thinking through the financial plan will improve your insight into the inner financial workings of your future salon. Remember, the numbers never lie so pay attention to what these numbers are telling you.

Appendices

Attach here your personal financial statement, sales rojections and cash flow statements, team bio's, location due diligence and other information that you may have referred to in the business plan but is not fully included in the BP.

Remember, the business plan is your road map for _your_ business. No one see's your future the way you see it. No one is clearer about how to get from one point to the next than you are. Be succinct with this plan. As you begin to draft this document, you will learn more and more about your proposed business and everything that goes into developing a successful hair salon. Keep this document current even after you have opened your salon. You should refer back to it anytime you need guidance for any aspect of the business. Remember, this is your plan for your business. Keep it alive. With failures so prevalent, be the success story. To be the success story, all your efforts will be required and this includes writing and maintaining a good, solid business plan.

Chapter Four

Step Two: The Numbers

I hear this all the time: "I don't do numbers" or "I'm not a numbers person" or "numbers scare me"! I say this simply is not true. We are all numbers people and all of us are numbers driven whether you know it or not. Think about when ordering your favorite coffee drink from Starbucks. Do you not specify the size of drink you order? "Tall, grande, venti"? Each of these sizes represents a number.

How about distance? Do we not all quantify how far we must drive or pedal or walk to get to work or school? And for those of you who drive, how much gas you pump to fill your tank and at what cost? For those of you who pedal or walk, do you not allow the appropriate amount of time to reach your destination?

Ever take your own pulse? Or see a doctor to check your blood pressure? Are you the oldest, youngest or only child in your family? How many seconds in a minute? How many minutes in your favorite T.V. show? Did you purchase a dozen ears of corn or only a half dozen? How long can you hold your breath under water? As you can see, we knowingly and unknowingly work with numbers every day, all day.

Let's think about some more numbers. Do any of these mean anything to you? How many guests did you service today? How many were color guests? Of all your guests today, how many pre-booked their next appointment? How many guests took retail products home with them today? How many of your guests returned? What is the average revenue generated per guest ticket?

Sweat the small stuff! What I mean here is, don't look at financials as an aggregate of revenues or an aggregate of expenses. You need to know where your revenues are being generated and how your money is being spent. Pay attention to the details; sometimes the very small details. As a young adult I was once told that "pennies make dollars" and in a small business, this saying has never been truer.

See how we begin to think in numbers and as an owner? The "numbers" of your future business must work, meaning you cannot operate indefinitely without making a profit, otherwise what's the point? The numbers of a salon are all over the map and include staffing, square footage (of the salon), number of chairs, total hours open, days open, salon productivity, sales projections, cash flows, balance sheets, cash on hand: each of these represents a number that is IMPORTANT to your ultimate success.

Become intimate with each number of your business. If you don't understand something; ask. Also, be sure to hire a hair salon qualified accountant. Don't cheap out and do your financials yourself or assume your "Aunt Mary" will do them for you for nothing! We recommend that you hire an accounting firm that is familiar with the inner workings of the hair salon. Not all accountants know the difference between technical and guest service payroll or know terms such as "back bar" or waxing. It's critically important to hire an accountant who understands your business.

The right accounting firm completely understands your business and what it takes to keep you financially sound. They will maintain your monthly profit and loss statements, balance sheet and benchmarks to be sure you are on track with your business.

So, as you are drafting your business plan, you should also be working on your sales projections and cash flows. Do these for the first three years of your business. S.O.A.R. is providing you with a detailed list of likely expenses at the end of this book. Your projected revenues and expenses will determine if your salon can or will be a viable business for you. If you were once a hair stylist, you will begin to transition your thinking as a business owner. You will begin to understand why we stated early on that as a salon owner, you will need to hang up your hair styling hat. In most cases it will be impossible to wear both hats so from the start, don't even try.

Remember this: The numbers never lie!! So be truthful and be conservative when developing these spreadsheets. And do them! More than a few major corporations have learned the hard, humiliating and costly truth. The numbers are the numbers and no amount of ignoring them or "fudging" them will make your salon healthier from a financial perspective.

The financial plan consists of a 36 month sales projection, a cash-flow projection, a projected alance sheet and a break-even calculation. Together they constitute a reasonable estimate of your company's financial future. More important, the process of thinking through the financial plan will improve your insight into the inner financial workings of your company. Remember, the numbers never lie so pay attention to what these numbers are telling you.

36 Month Sales Projection

Many business owners think of the 36 month sales projections as the focal point of their business plan. This is where you put it all together in numbers and get an idea of what it will take to make a profit and be successful. Your sales projections will come from a sales forecast in which you project service and retail sales, cost of goods sold, expenses, and profit month-by-month for one year. Profit projections should be accompanied by a narrative explaining the assumptions you used to estimate company income and expenses. Also, keep good notes on your research and assumptions, so that you can explain them later if necessary, and also so that you can go back to your sources when it's time to revise your plan.

Projected Cash Flow (Cash is KING!!)

If the profit projection is the heart of your business plan, cash flow is the blood. Businesses fail because they cannot pay their bills. Every part of your business plan is important, but none of it means a thing if you run out of cash.

The point of the cash-flow worksheet is to plan how much you need before startup, for preliminary expenses, operating expenses, and reserves. You should keep updating it and using it afterward. It will enable you to foresee shortages in time to do something about them— perhaps cut expenses, or perhaps negotiate a loan. But foremost, you shouldn't be taken by surprise. There is no great trick to preparing it: The cash-flow projection is just a forward look at your checking account. This spreadsheet will track all revenues and expenses of a hair salon. Understand each line item in this spreadsheet. Not doing so will spell certain disaster.

You should also track cash outlays as starting cash at the top of the first column of the first year. You should have already researched those for your startup expenses plan. Your cash flow will show you whether your working capital is adequate. Clearly, if your projected cash balance ever goes negative, you will need more start-up capital. This plan will also predict just when and how much you will need to borrow. It's critical to get your arms around your needs before you need the cash.

Again, be sure to explain your major assumptions, especially those that make the cash flow differ from the *Sales Projections*. For example, are you selling gift cards? Do you sell other products that are not quantified within the sales projection part of the spreadsheet? When you buy inventory, do you pay in advance, upon delivery, or much later? How will this affect cash flow? Are some expenses payable in advance? When? Are there irregular expenses, such as quarterly tax payments, maintenance and repairs, or seasonal inventory buildup that should be budgeted? Don't forget payroll. It will always vary.

Loan payments, equipment purchases, and owner's draws usually do not show on profit and loss statements but definitely do take cash out. Your spreadsheet needs to have all of these and more.

Opening Day Balance Sheet
A balance sheet is one of the fundamental financial reports that any business needs for reporting and financial management. A balance sheet shows what items of value are held by the company , called assets, and what its debts are, called liabilities. When liabilities are subtracted from assets, the remainder is owners' equity. Again, I advise that you hire an accountant who fully understands the hair salon industry.

Benchmarking
Your business is open, revenues are generating and the bills are being paid. Now it's time to measure your business from a financial perspective and this is called Benchmarking. Benchmarking is how you will measure the health of your salon. It's how you will keep track of all expenses as they pertain to your revenues. If the business plan is your road map, benchmarking are the gauges to the business you are driving.

Benchmarking keeps you apprised of the financial health of your salon. By definition: **Benchmarking** *is the process of measuring an organization's internal processes then identifying, understanding, and adapting outstanding practices from other organizations considered to be* ***best-in-class***. Benchmarking is a systematic process for identifying and implementing best practices within your salon.

As an example, how much back bar are you using each month against service revenues? 3%, 10%, 20% ? Just so you know, the industry benchmark is 5% or less of your service revenues. If you are not within that benchmark and are higher, then you are giving money away. This could mean that color bowls are being over filled or stylists are over zealous of their use of shampoo and conditioner at the shampoo bowl. Or, it could mean that your prices are too low. The bottom line is if you don't measure then you don't know and if you don't know then you can't fix problems and in turn, operate the very best salon that you can operate.

All successful businesses, not just salons, use benchmarking as a tool by which to learn and improve upon their business. By using this tool you can now maximize the potential of your salon. Benchmarking keeps you attuned to the fluctuations of your business allowing you the timely opportunity to fine tune your systems.

Benchmarking is a service your accounting firm should be providing for you each month. It's up to you, however, to provide that accountant the necessary data that will make benchmarking an accurate means to measure your business. This means keeping good records of every financial aspect of the salon. Remember, this is YOUR business. Run it with a great amount of alacrity and determination.

Other Important Numbers

You've now created a 3-year sales projection and cash flow spreadsheet. You have a better understanding of the balance sheet and benchmarking. So what other numbers are important to understand? Here is one for you to consider: Debt. How well do you understand debt? What it is? What it is for? And how it can be the death of your new salon?

We all have a simple understanding of what debt is. The dictionary definition is "something typically owed, typically money". This is true but are you fully aware of all your debt? Before you even begin the quest for funding to open your salon, make a list of all your personal debt. This could include credit card payments, car payments, student loan payments, personal loans, personal guarantees, alimony, child support or even tax payments. One form of debt that isn't always understood   is personal guarantees. A personal guarantee is that guarantee for all the debt owed for the term of the agreement. An example of this is apartment rent. You might pay $1000 per month rent, however if you signed a 12 month lease, your total debt is $12,000, not $1000.

When listing debt, create three columns. The first is the name of the debtor such as the name of the credit card company. The second column lists monthly debt such as what your monthly rent is and the last column lists long term debt. Long term debt would include the balance on a loan, such as on a car or home; it will include the amount guaranteed for rent, such as you would have signed for an apartment or commercial lease. Be sure to add these numbers up at the bottom. This sheet will become a part of your personal financial statement at least from the stand point of your personal debt.

If you are over-burdened with debt, it will be increasingly difficult to acquire the necessary funding for your salon, at least through traditional means such as bank loans or third party leases. Debt, in the form of loans, can be a great business and personal tool for the benefit of your new salon, but too much of debt will become problematic.

Chapter Five

Step Three: Establish your Salon...Legally!
You have now determined that you will forge ahead with your new salon. It's now time to establish this entity as a legally registered business within your state and locality. But what kind of legal entity should you be and how do you form it? As you begin to work towards forming your legal business entity, you should also consider hiring your accounting firm and attorney if you've not already done so.

Although I am not a real fan of paying someone to do something you might be able to do on your own, these two professions will ultimately save you money and keep you on track with your business. Remember, your goal is to succeed so assemble and surround yourself with a team of people who "have your back".

Your accountant will help keep you solvent or "in-business" and your attorney will be your business confidant. Attorneys, unlike accountants, are legally bound to confidentiality through attorney/client confidentiality agreements. The only reason I mention this at all is if you have any "secrets", share them with your lawyer, NOT your accountant. Your accountant is not protected under any sort of confidentiality agreement and therefore will never be privy to private information beyond the numbers of your salon. Hopefully, however, you have no secrets to worry about.

Most of the information I am providing has been gleaned from the Small Business Association web site and from personal experience. It will be up to you and your accountant as to what legal entity is most suitable for you and your salon.

Form the Legal Entity of Your New Hair Salon
Now that you have decided to own your hair salon, whether it is a franchised hair salon or your very own, independent business, you will need to create the business entity, also known as your corporation, your partnership, etc. This is when you will register your business with the state the salon will be located and give it a legal structure. There are several different kinds of business enterprises you can form and you should consult with your accountant and/or your attorney to determine which type is best suited for you and your business. The most common

forms of business enterprises in use in the United States are the sole proprietorship, general partnership, limited liability company (LLC), and corporation. Each form has advantages and disadvantages in complexity, ease of setup, cost, liability protection, periodic reporting requirements, operating complexity, and taxation. Also, some business forms have subclasses, such as the C Corporation or S Corporation. Choosing the right business form requires a delicate balancing of competing considerations. Learn how to select, plan, and organize the business form that is a perfect fit for you and your hair salon.

The Sole Proprietorship

The sole proprietorship is the simplest business form under which one can operate a business and is very common for the sole hair salon owner. The sole proprietorship is not a legal entity. It simply refers to a natural person who owns the business and is personally responsible for its debts. A sole proprietorship can operate under the name of its owner or it can do business under a fictitious name, such as "Nancy's Hair Salon". The fictitious name is simply a trade name--it does not create a legal entity separate from the sole proprietor owner.

The sole proprietorship is a popular business form due to its simplicity, ease of setup, and nominal cost. A sole proprietor need only register his or her name and secure local licenses, and the sole proprietorship is ready for business. A distinct disadvantage, however, is that the owner of a sole proprietorship remains personally liable for all the business's debts. So, if a sole proprietor business runs into financial trouble, creditors can bring lawsuits against the business owner. If such suits are successful, the owner will have to pay the business debts with his or her own money.

Advantages of the Sole Proprietorship

- Owners can establish a sole proprietorship instantly, easily, and inexpensively.
- Sole proprietorships carry little, if any, ongoing formalities.
- A sole proprietor need not pay unemployment tax on himself or herself (although he or she must pay unemployment tax on employees).
- Owners may freely mix business and personal assets.

Disadvantages of the Sole Proprietorship

- Owners are subject to unlimited personal liability for the debts, losses, and liabilities of the business.
- Owners cannot raise capital by selling an interest in the business.
- Sole proprietorships rarely survive the death or incapacity of their owners and so do not retain value.

The Partnership

A partnership is a business form created automatically when two or more individuals engage in a business enterprise for profit. "The association of two or more persons to carry on as co-owners of a business for profit forms a partnership, whether or not the persons intend to form a partnership." A partnership--in its various forms-- offers its multiple owners flexibility and relative simplicity of organization and operation. In limited partnerships and limited liability partnerships, a partnership can even offer a degree of liability protection.

Partnerships can be formed with a handshake--and often they are. However, I don't recommend it. esponsible partners will seek to have their partnership arrangement made official in a partnership agreement, preferably with the assistance of an attorney. Because partnerships can be formed so easily, partnerships are often formed accidentally through verbal agreements. A partnership is formed whenever two or more persons engage jointly in business activity to pursue profit. I have suggested to many future business partners that they might consider couples counseling before going into business together. Make sure you can work together through thick and thin; good and bad times.

Remember this. If you are going into business with someone, be sure you really know that person or persons extremely well. Do your philosophies mesh? Do you like one another? Is this a person you want to really, genuinely be with all the time? More businesses are sunk because the partners, who were once such great friends, became intolerant of one another and therefore all the best laid plans have disappeared.

I don't recommend operating a partnership without a written partnership agreement. Because of its informality and ease of formation, the partnership is the most likely business form to result in disputes and lawsuits between owners--verbal partnership arrangements are usually the reason.

The cost to have an attorney draft a partnership agreement can vary between $500 and $2,000, depending on the complexity of the partnership arrangement and the experience and location of the attorney.

Advantages of the Partnership
- Owners can start partnerships relatively easily and inexpensively.
- Partnerships do not require annual meetings and require few ongoing formalities.
- Partnerships offer favorable taxation to most small businesses.
- Partnerships often do not have to pay minimum taxes that are required of LLCs and corporations.

Disadvantages of the Partnership
- All owners are subject to unlimited personal liability for the debts, losses, and liabilities of the business (except in the cases of limited partnerships and limited liability partnerships).
- Individual partners bear responsibility for the actions of other partners.
- Poorly organized partnerships and verbal partnerships can lead to disputes among owners.

Limited Liability Company (LLC)
The LLC is often described as a hybrid business form. It combines the liability protection of a corporation with the tax treatment and ease of administration of a partnership. As the name of this business entity type suggests, it offers liability protection to its owners for company debts and liabilities.

Simplicity and Flexibility
While LLCs are relatively new creations of state legislatures, corporations are truly ancient and today's corporate law still carries some unwanted baggage. The basic principles of American corporate law have not changed significantly in centuries. Probably the single

greatest disadvantage of the corporate form is the burdensome range of formalities that corporate managers must observe.

The LLC changed all that. The LLC offers the liability protection benefits of the corporation without the corporation's burdensome formalities. It is this simplicity that has made the LLC an instantly popular business form with businesspersons operating smaller companies and in general, an ideal structure of the new hair salon owner. And if you out grow your business in such a way that an LLC is no longer the appropriate structure for your salon, then it's simple to convert an LLC into a corporation

Advantages of the LLC
- LLCs do not require annual meetings and require few ongoing formalities.
- Owners are protected from personal liability for company debts and obligations.
- LLCs enjoy partnership-style, pass-through taxation, which is favorable to many small businesses.

Disadvantages of the LLC
- LLCs do not have a reliable body of legal precedent to guide owners and managers, although LLC law is becoming more reliable as time passes.
- An LLC is not an appropriate vehicle for businesses seeking to become public eventually, or to raise money in the capital markets.
- LLCs are more expensive to set up than partnerships.
- LLCs usually requires annual fees and periodic filings with the state.
- Some states do not allow the organization of LLCs for certain professional vocations.

Corporations
A corporation has perpetual life and is a legal entity that is formed under the laws of the state by which it is formed. When shareholders pass on or leave a corporation, they can transfer their shares to others who can continue a corporation's business. What this means that any of your shareholders can sell or transfer their shares to another individual or legal entity. A corporation is owned by its shareholders, managed by

its board of directors, and in most cases operated by its officers. The shareholders elect the directors, who in turn appoint the corporate officers. In small corporations, the same person may serve multiple roles--shareholder, director, and officer.

Corporations are ideal vehicles for raising investment capital. A corporation seeking to raise capital need only sell shares of its stock. The purchasing shareholders pay cash or property for their stock, and they then become part owners in the corporation. Of course, the sale of corporate stock is heavily regulated by the U.S. Securities and Exchange Commission and by state securities laws so be aware of this. Corporations must meet annual reporting requirements in their state of incorporation and in states where they do significant business.

This kind of structure can be cumbersome for the small hair salon owner.

Advantages of the Corporation
- Owners are protected from personal liability for company debts and obligations.
- Corporations have a reliable body of legal precedent to guide owners and managers.
- Corporations are the best vehicle for eventual public companies.
- Corporations can more easily raise capital through the sale of securities.
- Corporations can easily transfer ownership through the transfer of securities.
- Corporations can have an unlimited life.
- Corporations can create tax benefits under certain circumstances, but note that C corporations may be subject to "double taxation" on profits.

Disadvantages of the Corporation
- Corporations require annual meetings and require owners and directors to observe certain formalities.
- Corporations are more expensive to set up than partnerships and sole proprietors.
- Corporations require annual fees and periodic filings with the state.

As you can see, there are differing business enterprise types available to you as you begin to structure your new hair salon business. As mentioned previously, you should consult with either your accountant or your attorney to determine which entity is best suited for your new endeavor. Once you have formed the legal entity, you will now also be required to file annual tax returns. Your accountant will remind you but it's your business and it's your responsibility to be sure that tax returns are filed for each year that you are in business.

Once you know the type of legal entity your salon will be formed as, you will be required to contact the department of the Secretary of State within the state you wish to open and conduct your business. It's possible you will need to submit more than a single name for your new entity in the event the name you have chosen (i.e. Serenity Salon) has already been chosen in your state. If you are a franchised salon, you will need to register the business under a name separate from the name of the franchised salon you will own (.i.e Nancy's First Business Venture). However, you may choose to follow that up with a D/B/A (Doing Business As). Franchised salons will have your registered business name d/b/a "franchise salon name". You can also create a d/b/a to give your salon that personal touch (i.e. Nancy's Hair Salon).

Once you have formed your legal entity and have paid the required registration fees, the next step is to apply for a Federal Tax ID number or your EIN (Employer Identification Number) for the business. This is the corporate equivalent of your social security number. Any business that intends to pay withholding taxes on employees, including themselves, is required to apply for and is issued an EIN. The EIN is issued to all businesses who apply for one and is a way the federal government to examine the status of any corporate or business enterprise inside the U.S.

To apply, simply go to this URL or Google Apply for EIN and complete the simple form that is required.

http://www.gov-tax.net

Keep in mind that the EIN does not signify the type of status a corporation holds such as being an LLC, S Corp or Corp. Your accountant will qualify you when he completes your annual taxes.

REGISTRATIONS

Each state has different registration requirements. To determine what your states registration requirements are **Google** the following for your state:

- Business registration (state name)
- Secretary of state (state name)

If necessary, find the telephone number for the secretary of state for your state and call them directly. Each state will have it's own business registration department. It is your responsibility to know which government entity or department you need to work with to complete your business registration. Before you can open your doors, it is imperative that you have been issued all necessary business registration licenses for your state, your county and your town. Not every county nor every town requires you to register.

Most states will require you to register your hair salon. This license is usually called the Barber/Cosmetology Shops and Salons license. Regardless of its name, it will be your responsibility to investigate your own state, county and town/city registration requirements.

If your town is incorporated and has a town government, you should call and speak with the town clerk and recorder's office to determine if there are any special registration requirements. Always document your conversation with time, date and to whom you spoke. Regardless if your town is incorporated or not, you will need to contact your county clerk and recorders offices to again, determine if there are any special registrations you will require to operate your business legally. All the above steps are extremely important. Never simply assume you do not require any of the above mentioned business registrations. This assumption will only hurt you and your business. Imagine your salon being shut down, even for a day, because you neglected to register the business fully. It's embarrassing and will hurt your new business. Take no chances. These are simple steps so be sure to take them.

Sales Tax License Registration

In addition to being issued a business license, you will also need to request a sales tax license. Although any service you provide will not be taxed, all products that you sell for retail, whether it's shampoo, makeup, hair brushes or jewelry, will be. You are required to charge your local sales tax as set by the state, county and any special district requirements.

To apply for a sales tax license you will need to contact the department of revenue for your state. This can either be a telephone call or via the internet. Regardless of how to contact your states department of revenue, you will need to complete the Business Registration form. You will need the following information:

- Registered company name
- If you are "doing business as" ("DBA"), you will need to provide this information
- What is your company structure? i.e. "C" Corp, LLC, "S" Corp, General Partnership, etc.
- Business address
- County that you are conducting business
- Business telephone number
- First date that you will be open for business

There will be more information required so be detail oriented when completing this form. Should you have any questions, contact your department of revenue directly. Someone will be able to assist you with any of your needs. It's important to get this right the first time. As it is with business registrations, you cannot afford to have your state shut your business down for a moment because you neglected this very important step in the process of opening your new hair salon business.

It is up to you to know what taxes and their percentages you are required to charge for retail sales. Generally, sales tax will only apply to sales of products that your guests take home with them. Currently, services such as haircuts, color, waxing, etc are not charged a sales tax.

On to insurance and liabilities. Liabilities are the potential problems that requires the insurances you need to protect you, your business and your staff should anything go wrong. These insurances include both liability and workman's compensation. Liability insurance protects you in many ways: from fire to personal injury within the salon. Workman's compensation covers injuries to your employees. Both of these insurances are required either by law or at least by your landlord and every lending institution. So what could go wrong? Plenty. Take those rose colored glasses of if by chance you put them back on.

Although the odds of something bad happening in the salon are low, you need to prepare for any possibility such as fire or a guest falling and getting hurt or a stylist badly cutting her knuckle while cutting hair. You just don't know and truth is, you rarely ever see these things happening (well, with the exception of stylists cutting themselves). And as I said before, any lending or investing institution will require you to be fully insured and so will your landlord. It's just common sense to fully protect yourself.

As for who should you use to insure your salon? Well, you can use almost anyone in the insurance industry, but I will advise that you go with a company that specializes with insuring hair salons. These kinds of insurance companies have truly dialed in on the risks of our industry and will dramatically reduce your total insurance costs. We all hate paying for insurance, but unfortunately we live in a litigious society, so be sure you are completely protected.

Chapter Six

Step Four: Dial in on the Right Location
This may sound like a cliché, but: LOCATION, LOCATION, LOCATION! There are a whole lot of reasons why location is so important to the success of your business. To begin, hair salons need to be locations of convenience, not destinations. Salons are not vacation destinations as many spas are considered. People don't want to feel like they need to head clear across town to a little strip center just to get their hair cut. So, as you begin your quest for the perfect location, find a trusted commercial realtor who can do an electronic search based on your initial criteria and start to show you locations within your community.

Rising fuel costs are forcing consumers to consolidate their stops. One stop shopping is becoming more and more prevalent. Put yourself in your guests' shoes. Gas costs the same for you as do all the other costs associated with your vehicle including maintenance and insurance. Would you not want to drive around as little as possible thus reducing your vehicular related costs? Time is important too. Think about the parent who needs to shop for dinner, get their hair cut/colored and make it back to school in time to pick up the kids. Time is an extremely valuable commodity and the salon owner who gets and respects this will find themselves light years ahead of their competitors. Be the guest centric salon.

Grocery anchored salons are the most successful, statistically, for just this reason. Grocery stores are a "must have" and having a hair salon adjacent to where your guests shop is a bonus and also a savings on your marketing dollars due to your visibility.

There is much to consider, however, regardless of where your salon will be located. Cost will be one of the biggest factors. As you learned from benchmarking, rent and the NNN needs to be at or around 6% of your gross revenues; much higher and your ability to succeed diminishes and rarely will that percentage ever be lower than the benchmark. Of course, you will have already developed a financial plan to estimate what a particular location will generate both in hair care services and in retail. Knowing your numbers through the development of reasonably accurate revenue generation proformas will help determine if you can afford a certain space or not. It will also provide you with sound data by which to negotiate a lease that would work within the framework of your benchmarks.

Demographics are also a very important piece of data. Is there a reasonable population of potential guests living within one, three and five mile radiuses from your new salon? Remember, no people, no guests. Know who your competitors are and where they are. You don't want to commit to a location only to learn after the fact that there are numerous salons competing for the same business as you. Knowing as much as you can about your competitors will also help you with your business plan and with how you will market to future staff.

Know as much as possible about the shopping center or building you are considering to put your new salon. Many people don't give this enough consideration, but how old is the center you are considering to locate your salon? There are a couple reasons you should know this. First, will you have higher maintenance issues on things such as your heating and ventilation systems, or plumbing or even the windows (do they leak air or water?). Second, is there a plan to renovate the center in the future? This can be good and bad. The bad is renovations will disrupt your business. The good, if it's a nice remodel, guests may be more apt to shop in this newer looking center and this could have a very positive impact on your business. A newly remodeled shopping center may also see new tenants moving in; again, good for your business.

One thing you must also request is a non-compete agreement. What you never want to have happen is to have a direct competitor move into your center with you. Many of the deep discount, franchise brand of salons will have non-compete agreements that will prevent other, similar salons from renting space in the center. These non-competes generally do not prevent mid or higher priced salons from moving into the center so if you are the salon filling that mid to higher end, you need to require the landlord to draft a non-compete agreement thus preventing your direct competitor from becoming your direct neighbor.

The right space will provide you with ample, close in parking, walk-by traffic and high visibility to shoppers already in the center, good signage opportunities, minimal or no competitors and a real bonus will be a nice property management company.

The location of your new salon is important. This location should be a "location of convenience." Your salon must be located where guests will have other business or errands and not be a destination location.

Site criteria:

- High traffic location
- Highly visible location (don't be your communities best kept secret)
- Easy access
- National grocery store anchor preferred or
    - Lifestyle shopping center or
    - Super Walmart or Super Target anchor locations
- Population demographic minimum requirement if 15,000 in a 3 mile radius
- Close in and plentiful parking
- Median Household income of $75,000 or more
- Rent to be within industry benchmark of 6% within three years

Once you have dialed in on the right location, share your location with friends, family and others to solicit their opinions. "Would you come to my salon if it were located here"? If your small focus group provides you with a "double thumbs-up" then it's time to negotiate a lease and this is where a combination of realtor and attorney come in. DO NOT attempt to negotiate a lease by yourself. Remember, the owner of the space is in business too and will attempt to charge top-dollar for the space. You need an expert in your court and those are your realtor and attorney.

When determining what rents and triple net you can afford (N.N.N.) go back to your cash-flow spreadsheet. Based on this location it's now time to really dial in on sales projections to determine if this space is a financially viable location. Remember, as a rule, per those industry standard benchmarks, your rent and N.N.N. should not exceed 6% of your gross revenues. My recommendation is that for year one, it should not exceed 10% of your gross revenues but by year three, as your revenues increase, your rent should represent not more than the 6% industry benchmark.

You are a hair salon, not a bar or restaurant. Salons are labor intensive unlike many other business models, meaning that labor costs are a large part of a salon's expenses and therefore what you pay in rent, as a percentage of your gross monthly revenues, will need to be significantly less. Be sure to let your realtor and attorney know how you have derived at a projected rent and N.N.N.

Location Due-Diligence Criteria
Use the following criteria to help you qualify facts about each location you consider

Location Town: *State:*
Cross Streets:
Anchor Store (s):
Age of Shopping Center and Anchor:
Adjacent Businesses:
Easy Access: YES   NO
Close and Ample Parking: YES   NO
Interior Space   End Space   Stand Alone Space
Square Footage:
Base Rent*:*   *per Square Foot*
NNN: *per Square Foot*
NNN Includes:
Term: _
Tenant Finish*:*   *per Square Foot*
Local Area Population: 1 Mile   3 Mile   5 Mile
Average Household Income: 1 Mile   3 Mile   5 Mile
Property Developer:
Property Management Company:
Contact Name:
Contact Telephone:_
Contact Email Address:
Competitors:
Brochure: YES   NO
Site plan: YES   NO

Recycle an Existing Location
If or when possible, a great way to save both money and time is to find an existing hair salon location that has closed and meets your minimum location requirements. Over the last few years, there have been a plethora of hair salon closings and many in great locations. If you are fortunate to find one of these; grab it!

You will save 30-70% or even more when it comes to build out and FF&E costs thus reducing by a significant amount the cost of your new salon. You can further market this salon as recycled, which might woo new customers to your salon by virtue of this simple, green initiative (recycling is a green thing to do).

Not every closed salon will save you money. Be sure that the salon you are considering is in good shape. Is the floor, lighting, HVAC, plumbing all re-usable? If so, then you will save enormously on construction costs as there may not be any other costs than decorating costs to make this salon into your salon. Did the previous owner leave behind any or all equipment? If so, can you use any of it? At least until your salon is cash-flowing positive enough to replace? If not, then of course you will need to purchase all the necessary equipment for the business.

Adapting a business into a similar business is not a new concept. It is this strategy that was implemented by Colonel Sanders of Kentucky Fried Chicken fame. This is a great way to get you going without having exceptionally deep pockets. Be sure, however, to adhere to your minimum location requirements because and as you know, where you are located is important to your ultimate success.

Build Out
You've secured your new salon location. It's now time to build your salon. There are several steps that you need to follow. The first is to secure an architect and a salon designer. Hopefully these will be the same people or within the same firm. Choose a local architect who understands local building codes and requirements. This is critical as different towns, cities, counties or states have different building codes and you must adhere to these local codes in order to receive your Certificate of Occupancy.

When choosing an architect, request three references and check each of them fully. Have them share with you some of the work they have done in the past. Make sure they have designed commercial spaces not just residential spaces. Codes differ and therefore the architect you choose must be aware of this. Find out also, all that is included with their fees. Do they charge a flat rate or an hourly? You really need to define these costs up front otherwise you might find yourself paying a lot more for less than you thought you were going to be getting.

Will the architect help price out the construction? Will they assist you with decorating and color? Can they advise you on the different types of lighting you should be using? Obviously, the more they do the more it will cost so have a budget in mind. Interview several architects and let each know that you are interviewing multiple architects. This puts each on alert and sends the message that you know that you are serious and have a clue about what you are doing. Make them respect you. Remember, this is your salon and who ever you hire, they work for you, not the other way around.

If you have decided on certain styling stations, whether wall mounted or free standing, be sure to let your architect know this. Also, will your shampoo bowls be wall mounted or free standing as well.

Save magazine articles or take pictures of salons you like and provide as much information to your architect as possible, especially if they have never designed a salon before. As for rough design, most distributors or manufacturers of salon furnishings will provide a simple design layout for you based on your exact space in exchange for your purchasing your equipment through them. This can save you money as well and you now have salon experts laying out the floor plan of your new hair salon.

Generally speaking, salons are large, open spaces and therefore design and construction costs are less than if you were building a spa or other space that requires many "closed-off" spaces such as treatment rooms or offices. Most costs will be tied up in your electrical, plumbing and HVAC (heating, ventilation, air conditioning). Decorating can also raise costs depending on your decorative intentions.

Once you have some preliminary drawings completed, you should now have enough to start pricing out the costs associated with building your new hair salon. The more work you put into this personally, the less cost. Obviously, if you hire a decorator and ask the architect to price everything out for you, costs will increase. But, this is still a conversation you should have with your architect. Timing is so important but sometime so difficult between signing a lease and building your salon.

Be sure before you sign your lease, that you have a relatively good idea of what the entire salon is going to cost you. A general rule of thumb is to take your total square feet and multiply that by $100. This will give you a close estimate what the salon will cost you inclusive of construction, design, FF&E, products and supplies. This assumes a very basic salon and not a recycled salon, which should cost less, nor a salon with top-end, high dollar finishes. There can be nothing worse than sign a lease and find that you have way underestimated the cost to build your new salon. Further to this, you should also have preliminary approval form a lending source, if you are not funding the project with your own capital, before you sign a lease. Once you have committed to a lease, you have committed to that space for the duration of that lease. Don't find yourself completely unprepared or unaware of what your new hair salon is going to cost you in real dollars. A landlord will not be so forgiving if you made a major mistake is knowing the cost of this project. A landlord with integrity will most likely not allow you to sign a lease without your cost estimate and financing already in place. But don't assume that every landlord is the same. Many are desperate to fill empty spaces and will do so at any cost, even if it means generating the belief that if funding doesn't come through, the landlord will let you out of the lease. Make no such assumptions.

The second step is to hire a general contractor to build your salon. Choose wisely. Check all references and heed the reports you get back. Your architect my refer contractors to you; just be sure to get at least three references and check each of them out carefully. Remember, this is your business and the last thing you need is a contractor that talks a big talk but is unable to fulfill your project fully and within budget.

The purpose of this portion of the document is to assist owners and salons in budgeting the costs of their salon build out (construction). The table below will list, for your consideration, most everything that will go into building out a new hair salon in a new space. If you are moving your salon into an existing hair salon space, then your costs and building requirements will be dramatically reduced. None of the items below should be new to an experienced contractor, however, there are certain aspects of the salon which might be new such as plumbing requirements for shampoo bowls, hot water requirements and electrical demands for each salon station.

Buildout Categories	S.O.A.R.	Buildout Categories
Ceiling Access Panels	Cabinetry throughout salon	Plumbing Rough
Electrical Rough	Core Drilling for plumbing and power	Framing
Exhaust system	Fire electrical and suppression systems	Drywall
Painting and texturing	Finish carpentry	HVAC System
Insulation interior walls	Lighting fixtures	Plumbing fixtures
Flooring	Security System	Telephone/Internet wiring
Trash removal	Permits	Signage
General contractor fee	Insurance	Surprises

As you review the table above, you begin to realize that construction, even of a simply designed hair salon, can be a major construction project. Each of these items is part of the salon. How much is already completed, such as in a recycled salon will vary but it's up to you, your architect and your contractor to go through each item, step by step to determine the overall scope of the project. As I have said over and over again, this is your salon, this is your business and the ultimate responsibility to be sure the project is completed correctly and within budget is all yours. Yes, you will surround yourself with experts, but ultimately, it is you who need be accountable for everything about your new salon. This is the biggest hat you will ever wear as an owner. Simply put, the buck stops with you and no one else. So always maintain a high level of integrity, accountability and responsibility with your new salon. It will pay off in ways you may not even understand just yet. And one other benefit is that you will sleep better when you go to bed each night.

Chapter Seven

Step Five: MARKETING-"I'm Over Here"!!
Books upon books and articles upon articles have been written solely on the subject of marketing and advertising. Some are specifically for the hair salon industry. What I will say is this: "Don't be the best kept secret in your community" and "don't throw good money down the drain"! Both of these statements are so true. As a business owner, it is now your responsibility to make your community, if not the world, aware that you have or are about to arrive. Marketing is the means by which you will make your community aware of not only your existence, but everything about your business including: services offered, hours, pricing, culture, products, etc (the list goes on). Marketing and advertising are the ways by which you will keep a constant stream of guests coming into your salon.

But both marketing and advertising can become a huge black hole. More money than you ever thought possible can be spent to advertise your new business with results ranging from amazing to nothing. Be careful what you spend, how you spend and where you spend it and the best way to control spending is to stay within your benchmark.

What is the difference between marketing and advertising? They are directly related but have their differences. Advertising is the piece of marketing that "advertises" your message through some sort of media outlet as I will describe later on. Marketing is the strategy behind your advertisements. Marketing is geared towards developing your message and understanding the needs of your guests then creating a campaign you will advertise.

Marketing is a critical component to the success of any business, salons included. Yet marketing can also cause the demise of many a business due to the potential of high costs and ego. Yes, EGO. If the most important word in the world is "your name" then the second most important word (or words) will be the name of your business. Everyone likes to see their name in lights, or in full page, four color glossy ads. But, at what cost and what will the return on investment be? Yes, marketing and advertising is all about the ROI or **return on investment**. And by the way, never let your ego get in the way of any aspect of your business. Remember that.

Marketing and advertising your business is all about bringing guests into your salon and it's therefore important to measure your ROI. Truthfully, you only want to spend your money where you will get the greatest results and highest ROI. As for the ROI, there is a simple formula for you to use.

ROI=(revenue earned from investment - cost of investment)/cost of investment

In simple terms; if you spend $2000 for a beautiful glossy ad in a locally read magazine but the ad only generates $3000 in gross revenues, you have an ROI of ($3000-$2000)/$2000 or 0.5. But if you spend $30 on 4 electronic News Letters and you generate $3000 in gross revenues, you have an ROI of a whopping 99x! As this example shows you, the higher the ROI the better for you and your salon. By measuring your return on advertising costs, you can be sure that your dollars are being spent intelligently and in the right place. There are many ways and an equal number of places to market and advertise your salon.

Whenever you advertise, always have some sort of call-to-action. Give whoever is viewing or listening to your ads a reason to visit you. Always track as well when the guest comes into your salon, where they learned of your business. Keep this information in your system. It will allow you to accurately track where your guests are learning about you.

Consistency is critical to advertising no matter where or how you advertise. Repetition is an important part of advertising. Through consistent advertising, you begin to build credibility within your community and establish your salon as familiar. Through this repetition, your guests will always have your salon in the forefront of t   h   e   i   r minds when they require any of the services that you provide. Repetition will help establish your salon and its brand within your community and help ensure a continual flow of guests into your salon.

Marketing should start the day you sign your new lease. Do something simple and cost effective such as a "Coming Soon" banner that is visible to anyone traveling near your new location. Make sure you have your web address (if you have one ready) and a telephone number on this banner. As you near your opening date, you will slowly ramp up the amount of advertising you will do. Remember, if no one knows about you, your grand opening may not be so grand.

Create flyers that you can post in the windows of neighboring business windows or at your local churches, gyms and other places where you will get some broad yet cost effective exposure. Let's squash the myth that you have to spend big bucks to make big bucks. Marketing and advertising can become a bottomless black hole as I have previously mentioned, sucking you dry of your cash if you are not careful.

There are many ways to advertise your business as I have described in the table below. Your advertising ROI will really depend on your demographics, which media is most followed, how often your ad will be viewable or heard, how often you run your ad campaigns (discounts usually given for long term campaigns or agreements).

When keeping costs in mind, consider the benchmark; advertising should not exceed 3% of your gross monthly revenues. Use this as a guideline. The exception to this benchmark will be when you first open your salon. You will clearly spend much more on a percentage basis. In part, because you're not yet generating reasonable revenues and also in part because you are trying to make a bigger splash announcing your new business. However, you still have a responsibility to the cash you have available to operate your business, so advertise intelligently. As I have said previously, advertising and marketing can be a big, black, deep hole when it comes to the amount of money you can spend. Be careful and cautious and completely aware when ad-selling sales people knock on your door and pitch you something that sounds great as it rolls off their tongues but in reality derives no direct benefit to your salon. Never be impulsive or fall prey "this is the last space we have" or "I need to know today so you can take advantage of such a great deal". Turn a deaf ear to those kinds of sales pitches. I promise, you will regret this kind of impulsive decision.

Media Type	Cost
Newspaper	Medium-Expensive
Glossy magazine	Very Expensive
Radio	Expensive
T.V.	Expensive
Direct mail	Medium to Expensive
Email Campaigns	Low-medium Expense
News Letters	Inexpensive
Social Media	Inexpensive
Web Site	Inexpensive -Very Expensive
Referrals	Inexpensive
Campaigns	Charity Events
Grand Opening	Holiday Events
Product Driven	Men/Women Event
Service Driven	Teen

Media

Let's consider the differing types of media for your salon. If your salon is in a reasonably large city or town, you will have many choices. If located in a more remote area or small town, your options for media will be more limited. Media ranges from paper to the air waves to television and to the Internet. Make a list of all media opportunities in your area and contact each to learn more about what they offer and at what cost.

Newspaper

This is fast becoming a defunct means by which the verage person gets their news or seeks advertising. Newspapers are getting thinner and thinner and in many areas, have disappeared all together, yet many publications are hanging on and therefore creating advertising opportunities for local small businesses such as your salon.

Some things to consider when advertising in a newspaper: How often does the paper run? Is it a daily, weekly or monthly publication?. You either want long shelf life or a killer deal if running ads on a daily basis. The problem with daily newspapers is that you "will" miss viewers all the time. If you run an ad on Wednesday, but I miss the paper then I miss your ad which is why I say to advertise daily, you better be getting a killer deal on the campaign.

Generally, however, newspaper advertising is expensive and becoming less and less effective. This isn't to say that with certain papers in certain areas advertising in a newspaper won't be effective and with a reasonable ROI.

Glossy Magazines

These kinds of ads are usually sexy and gorgeous! These kinds of ads are almost always VERY EXPENSIVE. Be careful here. For most independently owned hair salons, this kind of advertising isn't an option due to the high cost to advertise. I have seen, however, several small salons spend a small fortune on this kind of advertising only to regret their decision later as there was little to no ROI on this kind of advertising. Do not let your ego control where and how you will advertise. Ego based decisions are stupid and will cost you your business. Generally, you should leave this kind of advertising to the deep pocketed national brands.

Radio

Like newspapers, radio is slowly becoming a media of the past with the advent of satellite radio and iPods in the car. Further, it's very much hit or miss as to who will hear your ads and when. Radio advertising can also be extremely expensive if on a major station at prime driving times such as morning and afternoon rush hour. Fewer people are listening the radio today than ever before in the past, therefore, this may NOT be the best media outlet to spend your hard earned dollars on.

TV

Cable TV has brought down the cost of advertising but has also diluted its overall effectiveness for us small guys. There are so many channels now to choose from to truly be effective. You need to spread your ads out over many channels and time slots. Additionally, you will have the cost to produce a professional advertisement. This too can become very costly and therefore leave you with little ROI.

Direct Mail

Direct mail is another means to market your salon but over the last several years has begun to lose its luster. First, it can be expensive to purchase the appropriate data base of qualified mailing addresses, you will need to design the piece that you intend to mail, then have it printed and lastly, pay the post office to drop that bundle of marketing pieces into one of those blue, mailboxes. Now think about when you go to the mail box and sort through your mail. If you are like me, it's very rare that I ever keep or even look at a direct mailer addressed to me. For me, it's junk and it therefore gets tossed and if this was your mailer; you just wasted a lot of money. Truth be told, this is another stupid way to spend your money. Just say no!

Email Campaigns

I'm going to say very little about this other than don't do them. This will entail you to use your email address or one you have set up using a third party provider such as Yahoo or Gmail. The problem is that most of these kinds of emails end up in your recipients Spam folder and are never read. Further, you could get yourself into trouble from the FCC or cyber police if you have not also included all "opt-out" information. Simply, don't do these. Instead, sign up with a news letter company such as Constant Contact.

News Letters (sent to the Guest's email)

Now you're cooking with gas by using a third party firm to handle all the legalities of sending out electronic, news letters. I am a big fan of this kind of marketing. It's very cost effective and usually has a very high ROI. That's a win, win for you and guess what? Your guests will grow accustomed to receiving these kinds of communications from you. Further, these rarely end up in a Spam folder and they have all the "opt-out" information at the bottom of the news letter and you won't have to do a thing. cool huh?

There are many companies out there wanting your business such as Constant Contact, Jango Mail, icontact, Campaigner and Graphic Mail to name a few. These companies can have you up and running within minutes and will cost you little to nothing. Wow! What a great ROI. There are two real caveats with news letters: first, be sure to collect email addresses and two, you must be consistent. Don't send a news letter out today then not again until a month from now. Decide how often you want to send these types of communications. In the beginning, send these out once a month at the same time each month, see how they work and you can always increase their frequency.

News letters are a great way to promote your salon, your staff, events, promotions, etc. Any of the previously mentioned programs are easy to set up and use which makes your life nice and easy. In every news letter, always include your salons telephone number (make it easy to read and find) and your salons web address. You should also have a link connecting recipients to your Face Book fan page as well.

Web Sites and Social Media
It makes sense to combine these two. We could have combined news letters here as well. We are now in the new millennium and the world has gone crazy over electronic media so don't be a dinosaur. Your new salon will need a web site, a Face Book fan page, a twitter account, Yelp and perhaps others. Think about this. Do you have a smart phone? Do your friends? Family? Colleagues? Most people these days can access a plethora of information from their cell phones, iPads and computers. This information will include your salon.

Don't be left out and don't be left behind. With the exception of a web site, setting up social media such as Face Book and the others are free. A web site can range in price, depending on the number of pages and how complex your site is. There are companies such as Go Daddy who provide tools so you can build your own site for as little as $200 per year. There are other web developers who would love to build you a site. As a business owner, you will get used to the fact that everyone will want to stick their hands in your pocket. it's up to you to decide where and how much of your money to spend. But a web site is critical these days to the ultimate success of any business. Be sure to have one and make sure it reflects your salon and the message you wish to share with the world. Web sites are good places to dive into the "why" you do what you do.

Your web site is now your online brochure and you can update it anytime you want. Think about that. No more expensive printing and graphics fees. Cool! As mentioned before, everyone is accessing information digitally and using a multitude if devices. Your website is a great way to step up your level of customer service by providing easy access to the information your guests want most. Your web will also present a professional image of you and your salon. This is important not just for your guests, but future staff as well. With so many potential salons to work for, stylists are more and more using the web to determine which salons are most suited for them. You web site is a great place to have online job applications. Make applying for a job in your salon simple and to to that, you need a web site.

Social media is the most cost effective means to promote your business. Free is always a good thing, especially when you can benefit financially from what you get for free. Through social media you will build a core group of supporters of your salon, which is essential to getting your business going and growing. This group of followers who follow you on Face Book or any of your other social media will continue to bring business into your hair salon and referring your salon to their followers from their social media. Think about how many friends you have and how many friends your friends have. Social media will also help you brand your salon.

Face Book, Yelp, Ping, Twitter, Yahoo, LinkedIn are all social media networks and all of them are available to you for FREE. Consider Face Book. This social network has over 700,000,000 active users (over twice the population of the United States). LinkedIn has over 100,000,000 active users. The point of sharing these staggering numbers with you is to make you fully aware of where the future lies with the Internet. Social Media is growing leaps and bounds and you do not want to stand on the side lines watching your competition sail past you. Learn all you can from every source on how to use these tools fully to your advantage. They are ever changing and ever evolving. If you stop learning, you will stop growing. As I've stated before, don't be a dinosaur.

Referrals

Referrals are the life blood of any business, especially the hair salon. Referrals are the most coveted testimonials. By providing an un-compromised guest experience you are almost assuring your growth because your guests will share this experience with their family and friends. Referrals are also one of the least costly ways of bringing new guests into your new or existing salon. This is one big reason why it's important to keep up with ongoing education for your staff. Make sure they know the latest color and cutting trends. You don't want your competition to pass you by. It's important as well to keep your salon neat and clean. The un-compromised guest experience is all encompassing. It begins with courtesy on the phone when booking an appointment then continues to how a guest is made to feel the second they walk into your salon. Be sure to always have some one up front to greet your guests. The experience continues with the service and how the technician listens to their guest and provides and exceptional service whether a cut, color or both. The experience also includes the gentle up sell of another service of a shine or deep moisturizing treatment at the shampoo bowl. The experience finishes by recommending the appropriate products to take home allowing the guest to achieve that same wonderful look and feel you just provided them. And don't forget to pre-book the guest so that they won't run the chance of not getting in when they need to see you again. Guests LOVE this and they will share the entire experience with everyone they know.

Never discount the power of extraordinary guest service and the experience it provides the guest. Now, more than any time in our national history, guests believe they are getting the short end of the stick. What I mean by that is, they perceive they are receiving less than they are paying for. this will not happen in your salon. consider this five-star service at perhaps three-star pricing. Your guests will be loyal to you and your team for as long as you continue to provide this level of service.

Something else guest love is knowing that they can see any of your professionally trained hair stylists without feeling as though they are betraying their primary hair care professional. Guests belong to the salon and it's important that your team understands this. It has nothing to do with "stealing" business from one technician and giving the business to another. It's all about accommodating the guest. And if the guest cannot see their usual stylist because that stylist is booked, out for the day or on vacation, then the guest can and should be allowed to book with any other qualified stylist without feeling guilt or embarrassed. And how cool is it when they run into their usual stylist and that stylist embraces that guest was able to see someone else without any level of angst from the usual stylist.

Referral business will be the best way to grow your business. This is just another example of why it's important as an owner to be present within your salon at all levels and not only from behind the chair. There are many, many things that go on every day within the salon that as the owner you need to be aware of, and most, if not all, will circle back to your salon being referred over any other salon.

Chapter Eight

Step Six: Giving, Community Support and Culture

I debated whether to include this topic under Marketing since it can and usually is a great tool for marketing your hair salon, but decided it needed a chapter all by itself. Giving is such a critical part of any business and it can be the life blood for almost any community on the planet. Giving is great for many reasons. First, it feels good. By giving you are helping some organization with its needs. Second, giving is a great way to promote and sustain your hair salon within your community. This is why you need to become the charitable leader within your community.

Giving is good for your business for many reasons; some are obvious, some not so obvious. When a business goes out of its way to hold a charitable event or volunteer for a local, national or global cause, the goodwill that you are imparting , comes back in enormous and subtle ways. It has been my personal experience that every time we have held a charity event or volunteered our time for a worthy cause, our local community supports our business. This follows Newtons third law of motion in that for every action, there is an equal and opposite reaction. In the case of giving, when you give, you get! Actually, the law doesn't completely pertain to giving because when you give, you get back way more than you ever gave. Regardless of who gets what, everyone wins.

Guests support businesses that support their community. This is a fact. When you support local, national or global initiatives that are important to your guests, those guests will always go above and beyond and out of there way to support your business. They will support you by showing up. They will support you by telling their friends and family to show up. Many of these guests that show up may be doing so for the very first time. It is your job as the owner of the salon and the job of your team to WOW these guests and earn their business through the extraordinary experience you will give to each. Giving and getting will become a perpetual cycle within your salon and this is what makes giving so great.

But where to begin? Like everything within your salon, this too can be encapsulated into a process. The first step is simply making the decision to give. Hold a charity event. My recommended process is to first determine which non-profit or non-profits you will support. What I have done successfully in the past as owner is, decide on one non-profit organization to support then let our team determine a second non-profit. By involving your team in this way, you will receive their full support. Charity events have to be inclusive of everyone in the business or as they say; "all hands on deck". In order for the staff to make the decision as to who they should support, each member of the team should offer to the non-profits they would like to have supported come into the salon and present themselves to the entire team. Allow the non-profit to explain more about their organization and why they should be the chosen non-profit organization to be supported for the salons charity event.

Several years ago at our day spa we decided to have a charity event to support the victims of Katrina. Everyone on the team was in agreement but I was approached by one of our young massage therapists who said that not getting paid for a days work was going to be tough on her. I offered her gas money and simply asked her to come in and support the event. She agreed and as it turned out, this was her first experience giving. At the end of the event, which was a complete success, we all gathered in our retail area and counted out the days revenues. This young woman was so touched when she saw that we had raised almost $7000 and watched us cut the checks that she would not take the gas money I offered her and walked out of the spa that night feeling better than she thought ever possible. Within the year, the same massage therapist decided to go to cosmetology school and left our spa. However, a year later she called me and asked if we planned another charity event. When I told her yes, she immediately asked if she could volunteer her time for our event, and she did. Giving is a very powerful elixir. You just need to give.

Once all non-profits have presented to the team, have everyone write down the organization of their choice, put their choice in a hat and when everyone has voted, tally the votes and the non-profit with the most votes wins. In the case of a tie, offer, as owner, to be the tie breaker or support both organizations, thus supporting a total of three at your charity event. This is a fun process and will open the eyes of everyone in the salon to non-profits that are in need of support. One criteria is that any non-profit that is chosen to be the beneficiary of your good will must, and I will repeat this, must be 100% on board with supporting the event and your salon. This is critical. You and your team will put a lot of time and effort into having this charity event, therefore, it's important to have the support of those you are supporting. This support must come in the form of being present on the day of the charity event and help spread the word about the event during the weeks before your big charity event.

With the support of the non-profits you will be supporting at your charity event, you will gain additional marketing opportunities through their contacts, relationships and efforts. Many of these individuals that the non-profit is marketing to may have never been to your salon and this is a good thing, from the stand point of gaining new guests that will hopefully become regular guests. The relationship you are establishing with the non-profits you will support must work for both the non-profit and your salon. Like most everything in your salon, this will be a team effort.

Like any event you hold at your salon, there will be lots of preparation in order to make the charity event a successful event. You will need to choose a date and decide exactly what to give. My advice is to give big. What that means is you need to donate 100% of all service revenues; 100% of any tips and as a way to encourage retail sales, donate a percentage of those sales as well. I also suggest that you create a basket of goods and services you can hold a drawing for and with those proceeds, you got it, donate 100%. It's important if you hold a drawing that you call it that and not a raffle. Raffles generally need to be registered with the state and truth is, that can be quite brain damaging so simply call it a drawing and you won't get into any legal trouble.

Giving big is a big deal. It shows your community that you are serious about your charity event and you will have a greater chance of selling the day out. It's hard to measure or quantify when you see businesses offering either small donations like 10 or 20% of sales, or even worse, of profits! This will not be you. You will be hugely generous and you will make sure your community knows it.

There are many ways to market your event. None of which should cost you much money. To start, contact all your local media. This will include newspapers, radio stations and local television stations. With all the same bad news in the press, the media is generally more than willing to publish your event and at no cost to you. Their stand is it's nice to hear some good news for a change and will be more than willing to get the good news out there. Other ways to market are to print flyers and place them all around your community; local gyms, churches, coffee shops, grocery stores and all local businesses near your salon. Create mirror talkers so that each guest that sits in your chair will know about the event. Make sure that everyone in the salon shares the event with every guest and encourage the guest to share the news with their network of friends and family. You will be amazed at how many people will ultimately support not just this event, but your salon in general and not just during the event, but all the time. Just remember to shout it out. Make the community completely aware of what you are doing and that your salon is the charitable leader of the community. This will endear your community to you which will help sustain your business through good and bad times.

Involve other local businesses with your event. They can get involved by either attending or serving complimentary food such as pizza and sandwiches, depending on who you can include. This makes your event even more robust and show's your support for your neighboring businesses, which will most likely turn into a great way to get even more referral business for your salon. Talk with your local trash removal company to see if they would be willing to set up recycling bins during the event. Anything you can do to give people a reason to stop by will ultimately be good for your business. Be creative with your thinking. Ask for suggestions from your team. Remember, the bigger the success of the charity event the better for your business and of course, the better for the non-profits your team has chosen to support.

On the day of the big event, make sure everyone is in on time; have a quick, motivational meeting and get the day started. Sell your heart out on retail and drawing tickets and remember to show every guest an un-compromised level of customer service. Remember, many of the guests you will have in your salon will be first time guests. Wow them and if you do, they will return and most likely will return with friends and family in tow. These return guests are great for your business and great for the non-profits you will support each year. This then becomes the perpetual cycle of giving and getting and in the end, the salon will always win. Remember, giving is an incredibly powerful elixir for everyone involved.

There are other ways for you to give as well. You and your team can volunteer your time at any number of non-profit organizations such as food shelters, the Elks Club when they serve free community meals or at an animal shelter. You can also support battered women shelters by allowing a certain number of women to come into your salon each month to receive a complimentary cut and/or color. What does your community need? What ever it is, be there in a way that makes sense for you, your business, your team and the organizations you will support. During these tough economic times, many of these non-profits are unable to fulfill their needs so any help that can be given, it will be greatly appreciated. You just need to commit to giving and helping; you, your business nor your team will regret it.

Culture, this is something you may have already given thought to or maybe not. Culture, however you define it, is an integral part of life and business. Culture is how your salon will be defined. It's how you will define the purpose and the meaning of your new salon. There is no such thing as the right or wrong culture. In fact, it's almost impossible to crisply define culture with words. However, anthropologist, James Spradeley defined culture like this: *"Culture is the acquired knowledge people use to interpret experience and generate behavior"*. As a definition, this is really good and will apply to your new salon. Think about these words "interpret experience and generate behavior". Regardless of how you might ultimately define culture for your business, by providing an un-compromised guest experience, will ultimately generate a behavior that is conducive to your business.

Who you are will greatly define your salon culture. If you are a giving person in life, you will be a giving person in your business. Culture in business becomes the way of life for the business which is why being consistent is so important. The culture of your salon includes everything you believe in including your values, your perceptions and your assumptions about life, people and the environment. The right culture for your business will bring out the best of everyone in your salon. It will help hire new staff as well; staff who will embrace the culture you have defined in your salon. This is also important for staff retention and will be a big defining difference between your salon and those you consider your competitors.

When you interview new staff it's important to share your culture with all new prospective employees. If new hires embrace your culture they will make not just better employees, but long term as well. Better employees tend to remain at companies longer and in the hair salon industry, it's a very good thing to retain your staff. When hiring new staff, you want natural "buy-in" to your culture. You don't want to convince someone that you are right for them; they need to convince you that they are "right" for you. When the right staff works within a business that shares similar, if not the same beliefs as the business itself, it almost always spells success when it comes to the synergy between the salon, you, the owner and everyone who works within the salon.

If you are a giving salon, which you should be, you will learn that three out of four people want to work for a business that does good. Giving needs to be a part of your culture; the paybacks to you as the owner are significant on many fronts. As we spoke above, you will hire the right staff. Please note the words, "right staff". The right staff will immerse themselves within your culture as if it were their own. They will inspire their peers, their guests and you. When giving becomes an entrenched part of your culture, yours guests will endear loyalty to you, your staff and your business. 86% of guests are willing to change brands in support of a brand that associates itself with charitable giving. Wow, now you have dedicated staff and loyal guests.

Culture; how you define it and make it yours is a clear pathway towards success. As with everything you do in your salon, you must be consistent. You must walk the talk of

Chapter Nine

Step Seven: Lights-Action-Camera

Are you ready? Remember, owning your own hair salon can be a fun and very rewarding experience if you are prepared. Assuming that things will just fall into place for you is no way to begin any type of venture whether it is a relationship or a business. Owning a business, much like entering a relationship requires planning, dedication, hard work, passion and a tremendous desire to succeed. It's tough out there and you need to fully comprehend that. Businesses fail and they fail all the time but not every business fails. There are plenty of very successful hair salons that have been in business for dozens of years or more. And although I don't know everyone's secret, the truth is, the steps and systems that this book lays out for you is the same or similar to what every successful business has done in or out of the hair salon industry. The only factor I have left out is luck as it's literally impossible to quantify and to predict the luck factor. That doesn't mean it does not exist, but you hardly want to use it as a metric for success. Further, anyone investing money into your venture will not want to gamble their hard earned money on luck. That's what the lotto and Las Vegas are for.

So as a recap of everything contained in this book, you need to follow certain steps towards opening and operating a successful business and these steps will begin with determining if owning your own hair salon is the right decision for you today. It's important to not only take your time with this decision, but do as much due diligence and homework on every possible aspect you should consider before delving into salon ownership. Look at the success side and the failure side. I know we don't want to think or discuss failure but you must recognize it as a highly probable end to most small businesses. So think about everything you will need to do to steer clear of the grim-reaper. Think hard about this: Why do you support certain businesses that you recognize as successful? Is it location? Quality of service? Price of service or product? What is it exactly that keeps you going back? Then think the same about other businesses you have been to but won't return. Is it because of its location? Ease of getting to the business? price? Service quality? Become your own secret shopper of competing salons. What would cause you to return or not to return. The very same things that will keep you either in support of or away from a business will very much be similar to what would keep someone away from the same business or more importantly, YOUR business.

What mistakes do you recognize that are made within other businesses that you have spent your hard earned dollars? There is no doubt you will make mistakes, however, it's important to learn from them. Even better if you can learn from some one else's mistakes.Whether these are mistake you have made or other businesses have made, learn from them and fix the processes that lead to the mistakes.

Build an effective and guiding business plan. I recently spoke at an event attended by over 300 business owners and when I asked the audience who has written a business plan, I was shocked to see fewer than 50% of the hand go up. It will be literally impossible to succeed unless you document your intentions within the business plan. This is a mission critical document that every business owner needs to draft before committing to the business they intend to open. There is no shortage of great business plan books, articles and actual plans themselves to follow. Remember, this is your business. Don't neglect drafting such an important document. It's your road map towards building a successful business.

And in conjunction with drafting the business plan, you need to start drafting sales projection and cash-flow spreadsheets. They say that the numbers never lie and to be clear, this is a very true statement. The only way to actually determine if you have a viable business, is to determine if your revenues can exceed your expenses. When I say viable, I mean a business that will generate enough revenues allowing you, as its owner, the ability to make a living. The numbers never lie but the only way you will know this is by developing sales projections as accurately as possible and then subtract out all the costs you will incur operating the salon. If revenues cannot or will never exceed expenses then the business model will not work, at least based on your projections. If you need help with your projections its a good idea to hire a salon centric consultant to help you derive at reasonably accurate financial numbers. Think about this, businesses fail because they can't pay their bills. They can't pay their bills when expenses exceed revenues. A successful business owner will therefore make sure that time is spent generating these kinds of spreadsheets before ever committing real dollars to any venture.

Once you know that you can open and operate a successful business, at least in terms of the financials then it's time to form your legal entity. which entity you choose is ultimately up to you and your accountant but you must do so before opening bank accounts or filing any other business registrations. It's important to then be sure you file all legal registrations. these include a sales tax license, salon registration

We've said it and you've heard it countless times: "Location, location, location"! Where you locate your salon can be a huge deciding factor on the salons ultimate success. In this day and age, being where the customers are already can be a very good thing, but be sure the cost of your location will fall in line with the industry benchmarks. High profile locations are always more costly but you will also spend much less on marketing and advertising so this could be an offset. Just do your homework. Look at the location, the traffic flows, what other stores or anchors are in the same shopping center and are there competitors near by. Be smart about where you locate your salon. Will guests find you? Will there be adequate parking? Can you afford the location? All of these will determine the right location for you.

Of course once you know where the salon will go, you will need to design and build it so start interviewing architects and builders. Be sure to express a proposed budget to both your architect and builder. No one likes surprises, especially the kind that cost you money and them, time. Not that it matters, but does either your architect or builder have salon design and construction experience? This is really a bonus for you if they do.

So that your new salon isn't the communities best kept secret, you will need to market the business and there are no shortage of ways to do this. What it will come down to is cost and return on your marketing and advertising investment. Keep in mind that marketing and advertising can become a big black hole for you financially so spend your money wisely. Ask other local business owners how nd where they market their business. It's ok to ask after all, if you don't ask, you won't get and in this case could be valuable information that could save you many dollars in failed marketing attempts. So much of what you do as a new business owner is learn and it's a good idea to learn from many different sources.

As a new, local, community based business, don't forget giving and charity. This could be the single most cost effective means to market and advertise your new hair salon. Generally speaking, local citizens will support those businesses that support them and their community. Be one of those businesses. Remember to give big as well. Make your contribution to charity a very meaningful and notable one. It will pay off. Giving will also help you to define the culture of your new salon. The good-will you build will help you grow a very positive reputation within your local community. Always walk the talk and always be consistent.

So, will this book guarantee your ultimate success? I wish it would but there are no guarantees in life and certainly none in business. Will this book help you build a successful and sustainable business? I surely hope so. Opening a new business is always filled with certain challenges. Knowing and understanding these challenges before you decide to own a business is a big step and a key step to building a successful business. It is that premise that this book is based upon. No doubt you will encounter something not covered in these pages but hopefully a foundation of responsibility and accountability and strength and confidence will have already been established so that when something you didn't expect happens, you'll be ready for the challenge. This book is dedicated to your success. May it be long, fulfilling, fun and prosperous!

Pledge for Business Success

I promise to work passionately every day towards succeeding in my business and in my life. I know that all I do or don't do will affect me, my team and the outcome and success of my business. I cannot blame anyone but myself if I do not succeed so I therefore promise to use each day to its fullest by giving the

Signature _____

Date _____

About Matt Walsh

Matt was born and raised in Chicago, Illinois before moving west to Colorado in 1996 and is the founding partner in MAKE It Education. Prior to joining the salon industry in 2004, Matt spent his professional career in the financial services industry as a Market Maker and later developed and sold a direct access trading system.

Matt had many connections to the World Trade Center and left financial services behind after 9/11, deciding to follow his entrepreneurial spirit and start his own business. In 2004, he and his wife opened a full service day spa. In its first year of operation, the spa was voted Best Day Spa and Best Customer Service business in Summit County, Colorado. The success of this business ultimately led to the formation of his next venture called Splish.

In an effort to grow Splish in the "down" economy, Matt began looking at existing salons whose doors were closed in order to re-cycle them. Matt quickly realized that there was no shortage of failed salons. Matt, along with a team of industry experts, established a new company called: MAKE It Education and a half day class called: *Business Brains for the New Hair Salon Owner* The purpose of this program is to reduce salon failures by providing common sense and applicable business knowledge to cosmetology students and anyone dreaming of owning their own hair salon.

Matt has spoken at several major Universities, many cosmetology schools, at Americas Beauty Show, in Chicago and at Paul Mitchell The Gathering. Matt has been interviewed by Winn Claybaugh for his Masters Audio Club.

Matt and his wife Andrea live in Keystone Colorado with their two children, Jackson and Meghan.

Visit Matt's web site for more information on available classes and other valuable information.

http://www.makeitedu.com

List of Probable Salon Expenses: They Add UP!

- Payroll (Styling, manager, guest services)
- Payroll Taxes
- Rent (Including NNN)
- Insurances (Liability and workman's comp)
- Professional Fee's (accounting/legal)
- Advertising
- Marketing (developing the advertising)
- Printing (menus, business cards, notes cards)
- Education (in and out of salon)
- Credit Card Fee's
- Bank Fee's
- Loan Payments
- Back Bar
- Cost of Retail Sold
- Maintenance and Repairs
- Supplies (Salon, office, cleaning)
- Utilities (Gas and electric)
- Phone and Internet
- Security System
- Meals and Entertainment (meetings, etc)
- Travel (Trade shows, etc)
- Magazine Subscriptions
- Franchise Royalty (if a franchise)
- Owners Salary
- Association Dues (PBA, etc)
- Salon Cleaning
- Promotional Fee's (In salon services)
- What else will you have?

Companies and Organizations Matt Supports

One Source Retail
www.onesourceretail.com

For custom salon furnishings, One Source is my only stop!

National Association of Eco-Friendly Salon & Spas www.naefss.org

For everything green and sustainable for your salon or spa. Join this organization for valuable information and insight

Harms-Software www.harms-software.com

The premiere provider of salon and spa centric systems.

Zaega Beauty www.zaega.com

Know what's in your products. Follow the industry expert.

Tremblay Consulting www.tremblay-consulting.com

Need help dialing in on payroll? Dave Tremblay is your guy. Don't let your payroll kill your salon!

180 Degree Education http://180ed.com

Need state approved continuing education? Here you go!

PBA www.probeauty.org

The Professional Beauty Association is loaded with all kinds of valuable information for your new salon or spa. Membership is worth the cost. Join today!

World Class Financial www.worldclassfinancialservices.com

The only accounting firm I "firmly" recommend for your hair salon. WCF will keep you on track, by the numbers.

www.ingramcontent.com/pod-product-compliance
Lightning Source LLC
Chambersburg PA
CBHW071622170526
45166CB00003B/1158